A to Z Nigeria

BY TAMRA ORR

children's press®

A Division of Scholastic Inc.
New York Toronto London Auckland Sydney
Mexico City New Delhi Hong Kong
Danbury, Connecticut

Consultant: Dr. Paul Kaiser, University of Pennsylvania African Studies Center, Associate Director
Series Design: Marie O'Neill
Photo Research: Caroline Anderson
Language Consultant: Yiwola Awoyale, PhD, Senior Researcher (Lexicography), Linguistic Data Consortium, and African Language Instructor (Yoruba), University of Pennsylvania, Philadelphia, Pennsylvania

The photos on the cover show the Emir of Dutse's palace (top left), a western lowland gorilla (top right), an Ekpo Society mask (bottom right), and a young Nigerian girl in traditional dress (bottom center).

Photographs © 2005: akg-Images, London/Werner Forman: 13; Alamy Images/Tim Graham: 9 left; AP/Wide World Photos/Das Saurabh: 36; Art Resource, NY/Werner Forman/Ethologisches Museum, Staatliche Museen zu Berlin, Berlin, Germany: 35 bottom; Bruce Coleman Inc.: 4 (David Madison), 5 top (Rod Williams); Corbis Images: 31, 38 (Paul Almasy), 15 right (Lynn Goldsmith), cover top right (Martin Harvey), cover center (Lawrence Manning), 7 (James Marshall), cover bottom right (North Carolina Museum of Art), 29 (Reuters), 6 left, 11 (Liba Taylor); Getty Images: 37 top (Pius Utomi Ekpei/AFP), 28 bottom (Issouf Sanogo/AFP), 32, 37 bottom (Jacob Silberberg), 5 bottom; Landov, LLC/Yoshiko Kusano/EPA: 12 bottom; Lauré Communications: 26, 28 top, 33; Marcia Kure/Chika Okeke: 15 left; Panos Pictures: 10 (Sara Leigh Lewis), 25 (Bruce Paton), 30 (Betty Press), 24 (Marcus Rose), cover top left, 12 top, 17 (Liba Taylor); Photri Inc./J.A. Cash: 23; PictureQuest/IT Stock Free: 21; Reuters/Ralph Orlowski: 14; The Image Works/ICONE/Ascani: 22; TRIP Photo Library: 6 right, 9 right, 27 left, 35 top (Juliet Highet), 18 (Mike Insall), 19, 34 (Jospeh Okwesa); Woodfin Camp & Associates: 27 right (Marc & Evelyn Bernheim), 8, 16 (Betty Press).
Map by XNR Productions, Inc.

Library of Congress Cataloging-in-Publication Data
Orr, Tamra.
  Nigeria / by Tamra Orr.
    p. cm. — (A to Z)
  Includes bibliographical references (p.   ) and index.
  ISBN 0-516-23666-0 (lib. bdg.)   0-516-24954-1 (pbk.)
  1. Nigeria—Juvenile literature. I. Title. II. Series.
  DT515.22.O77 2005
  966.9—dc22   2005006999

1 2 3 4 5 6 7 8 9 10 R 14 13 12 11 10 09 08 07 06 05

■ Contents

Nigeria's giant forest hog is the largest hog in the world.

Animals

Tall giraffes, yawning lions, and striped zebras once roamed freely under Nigeria's hot sun. Today, most of these animals are found only in wildlife parks.

Pygmy hippos

One unusual animal in Nigeria is the giant forest hog. It was not discovered until 1904. At 6.5 feet (2.0 meters) long and 600 pounds (272 kilograms), it is the largest hog in the world.

Lowland gorillas were once thought to be **extinct,** but two small groups live in southeastern Nigeria. Although these gorillas are protected by law, they are still hunted illegally.

Lowland gorilla

Nigeria is also home to an odd-looking creature called the pygmy hippopotamus. The pygmy hippo is only about 3 feet (1 m) tall and weighs less than 600 pounds (272 kg). Regular hippos weigh between 5,000 and 7,000 pounds (2,268 and 3,175 kg)!

Nigeria's royal palaces
are works of art.

The Central Mosque in Lagos

Buildings

Nigeria has a wide variety of buildings that include traditional mud-walled homes, beautiful **mosques** and royal palaces, and modern office buildings.

In northern Nigeria, the Emir's Palace in Kano was built more than 150 years ago. It is an Islamic-style building, with an **ornate** gateway that is decorated with a variety of **geometrical** designs.

Many Ijọ people build their homes on stilts because they live near creeks and swamps. In rural areas, many Yoruba people have homes that are made of mud bricks and have bamboo roofs.

Cities

One of Nigeria's many bustling, crowded markets

The bustling coastal city of Lagos is the largest city in Africa and one of the largest cities in the world. More than 10 million people call Lagos home. Until 1991, Lagos was Nigeria's capital. It is still Nigeria's main port.

Nigeria's second-largest city is Ibadan. Ibadan is an important trade center with several large, loud, and crowded markets. The Dugbẹ market is the biggest and is filled with the sounds of people bargaining. The Oje market sells hundreds of different kinds of cloth, while the Bọde market specializes in beads.

Kano is a favorite place for tourists. It has many attractions, including the Central Mosque and the Emir's Palace.

Nigerian clothing is bright and colorful.

Dress

Nigerians wear a wide variety of clothing. Yoruba men often wear an *agbádá*, a long gown that goes over a *bùbá*, or tunic, and pants. Some wear a cone-shaped hat, or fez, on their heads. Women may wear long printed skirts and tops called "up and down." In the north, some women wear long, dark gowns to cover their bodies and use veils to cover their faces. Many people also wear Western-style clothing.

Nigerian women are noted
for their elaborate braids.

Nigerian chief and horse in ceremonial dress

Ṣòkòtò

(shoh-koh-toh)
are loose trousers, with
a bùbá, or tunic.

Some people still create ceremonial masks for special occasions.
These masks are made from leather or wood and are decorated
with teeth, nails, hair, and fur.

In Nigeria, weaving braids into an elaborate pattern is a longtime
tradition. Braids can be found in some of the country's oldest
sculptures. Women and girls braid one another's hair or go to a
salon for the fanciest designs.

Palm oil worker

Exports

Nigeria produces an amazing 2 million barrels of crude oil every day, but it produces other kinds of oil as well. For years, one of Nigeria's biggest exports has been palm oil. Palm trees grow from Calabar in the east to Ibadan in the west. These palms have football-sized bunches of reddish-orange fruit. The fruit is pressed, and its oil is exported to countries around the world. The oil is used in cooking and can be found in everything from pizza to soap.

Recently, peanut oil has been catching up with palm oil. Peanuts are grown in Nigeria's northern **savannas.** They are harvested, crushed, heated, and pressed to get their oil. Like palm oil, peanut oil is used for cooking and making a variety of products.

Puff-Puffs Recipe

WHAT YOU NEED:
- 2 cups flour
- 2 cups water
- 1/2 cup sugar
- 2 teaspoons yeast
- Vegetable oil
- Powdered sugar

HOW TO MAKE IT:
Mix flour, water, sugar, and yeast together until smooth. Let rise for 2 1/2 hours, and then roll the dough into small balls. Pour 2 inches (5 centimeters) of oil into a pan and turn on low heat. When the oil is hot enough that it splatters if you flick a drop of water in it, spoon in one of the dough balls. Fry for a few minutes until the bottom side is golden brown. Turn over and fry the other side for a few minutes. Use a large spoon to remove the dough ball. Place on a paper towel to soak up the excess oil. Roll in powdered sugar.

Food

Some of the most popular foods in Nigeria include corn, yams, rice, black-eyed beans, and **plantains.** Rice is used in many different dishes, including fried rice and coconut rice.

Puff-puffs are Nigerian doughnuts sold by street vendors. Ask an adult to help you make puff-puffs using this recipe.

Nigeria's Parliament House in Abuja

Government

President Olusegun Obasanjo

For many years, Nigeria was controlled by **dictators** and the military. Today, Nigeria is a democratic country. This means the people elect their leaders by voting. Nigeria's Parliament House can be found in Abuja, the capital city. Its bright green dome and roofs contrast with the whiteness of its walls. These colors echo those found in the national flag.

Since 1999, the leader of the country has been President Olusegun Obasanjo. He is a Yoruba and was born near the city of Lagos. Obasanjo was reelected to another four-year term in 2003.

12

History

Nok terra-cotta sculpture

People often get glimpses into the ancient past through discoveries made in the present. In 1928, some **terra-cotta** sculptures were found by Nigerian tin miners. The sculptures were in the shape of human heads, snakes, and other animals. Some were only 1 inch (2.5 cm) tall. Others were life-size! They date back at least 1,500 years.

Archaeologists named the culture that created these sculptures Nok, after the town in which the sculptures were found. By studying the sculptures carefully, experts have learned much about what life was like in Nigeria long ago.

Important People

Many artists are from Nigeria. One of the most famous is the writer Wole Soyinka, who won the Nobel Prize for Literature in 1986. Chinua Achebe is another talented author. He has written more than twenty books. His novel *Things Fall Apart* is one of the best-known books ever written about Africa.

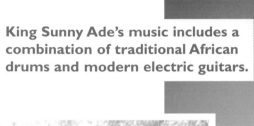

Marcia Kure is a well-known and acclaimed Nigerian artist.

Marcia Kure is a painter whose works are inspired by the simple colors and shapes of cave paintings.

One of Nigeria's most popular musical artists is the singer, guitarist, and **composer** Yoruba King Sunny Ade. He plays a type of African music called *jùjú,* which uses a combination of traditional drums and electric guitars. Fela Anikulapo Kuti is another important Nigerian singer, musician, and composer. Before he died in 1997, he pioneered a jazzy kind of music known as Afro-Beat.

Nigerian farmers work long hours on small plots of land.

Jobs

About half of all Nigerians are farmers. Some grow rice, yams, and corn, while other raise goats, sheep, and poultry.

Some Nigerians are teachers, government workers, and hotel and restaurant staff. Some make crafts such as leatherwork, jewelry, and pottery. Many Nigerians earn what money they can by parking cars or selling snacks to people stuck in traffic.

Keepsakes

Drums are very important in Nigerian culture. Musicians play a variety of drums in parades, festivals, weddings, and concerts. Images of drums have even been found on ancient artifacts.

Ayò is a popular game throughout Africa. It has many different variations and has been played for hundreds, perhaps thousands, of years. The game Mancala is a version of Ayò.

Dùndún

(doon-DOON) is a type of Nigerian drum.

Nigerian musicians and their drums

17

This aerial view shows a flooded Nigerian swamp.

Land

Nigeria has swamps and lagoons, forests and farmland, hills, valleys, and savannas. The highest point is Dimlang Peak, soaring 6,700 feet (2,040 m) up into the sky.

Traditional boats along the Niger River

The Niger River flows through much of Africa, including Nigeria. The Niger is 2,600 miles (4,183 kilometers) long and is sometimes called the Strong Brown God because of the **silt** that colors its water. The mighty river provides water, fish, and transportation for millions of people.

In 1968, the Kainji Dam was built across the Niger. When it was finished, it created a new lake that was 90 miles (145 km) long. Almost 50,000 people had to be moved when their old homes were covered with water. Today, the dam generates electricity for many Nigerians and is a major fishing ground.

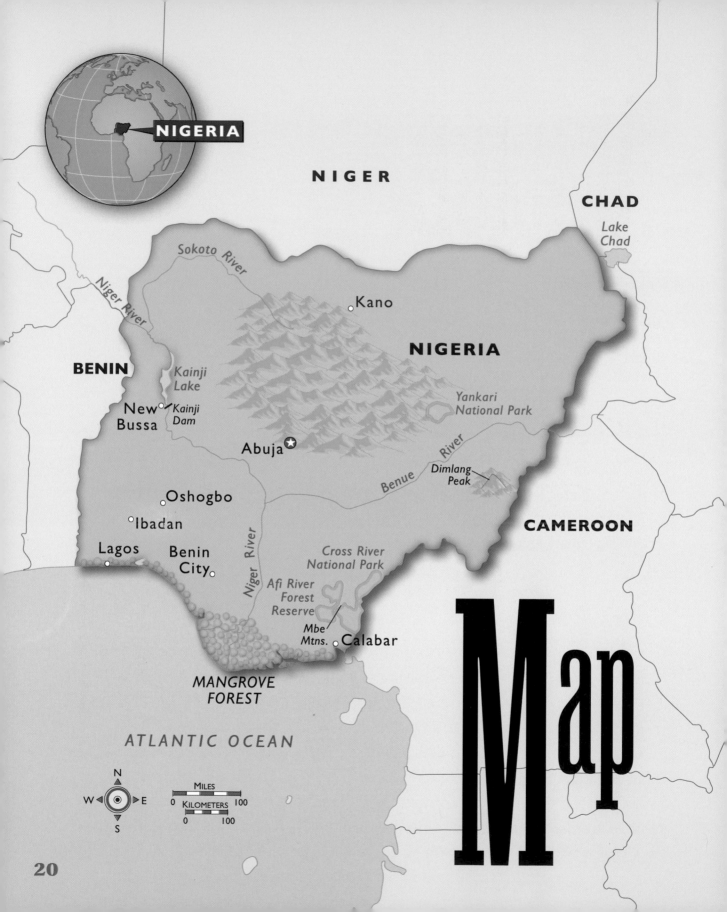

NIGERIA

NIGER

CHAD

Lake
Chad

Sokoto River

Niger River

Kano

NIGERIA

BENIN

Kainji
Lake

Yankari
National Park

New
Bussa

Kainji
Dam

Abuja

Benue River

Dimlang
Peak

Oshogbo

CAMEROON

Ibadan

Lagos

Benin
City

Niger River

Cross River
National Park

Afi River
Forest
Reserve

Mbe
Mtns.

Calabar

MANGROVE
FOREST

ATLANTIC OCEAN

N
W   E
S

MILES
0   100
KILOMETERS
0   100

Map

Nation

Can you imagine being given the chance to create your nation's flag? That is what happened in Nigeria in 1958. A huge contest was held, and more than two thousand people turned in their designs for a new flag. The winner was a student named Michael Taiwo Akinkunmi.

The flag has three vertical stripes of equal size. The two green ones stand for agriculture, while the white stripe in the middle symbolizes unity and peace.

Koma people

Only in Nigeria

Hidden at the base of the mountains of eastern Nigeria and neighboring Cameroon live the Koma people.

The landscape of the Koma people's homeland is quite dramatic.

No one in the outside world knew about the Koma until they were accidentally discovered in the 1980s. The Nigerian government worked hard to introduce the Koma to the rest of the country. Government workers helped dig wells and build roads. But today, the Koma still prefer an isolated, separate life.

The Yoruba people are one of
Nigeria's main ethnic groups.

People

Nigeria's population is more than
130 million people. It has the largest
population in Africa. There are some
250 ethnic groups and at least 200
different languages.

Festival time in Hawa

There are three main ethnic groups in Nigeria. The Hausa-Fulani live in the north and are mostly Muslim. The Yoruba live mainly in the southwest and are a blend of Muslim and Christian. The Ìgbò are mostly Christian and have traditionally lived in the southeast, although many have moved to other places to find work.

Some Nigerian languages are tonal languages. This means that one word can have many different meanings, depending on how it is spoken. For example, when people of the Yoruba ethnic group say "ko̩" it means "to learn" if said in a high tone, "to write" in a middle tone, and "to refuse" in a low tone.

Nigeria's rainy season brings huge amounts of water.

Question What's the weather like today?

Harmattan

(har-ma-TAN)
is a cold, dry wind in West Africa that often carries sand with it.

In Nigeria, the answer to that question depends on only one thing, rainfall. Instead of four seasons, Nigeria has two: dry and wet. In the dry season, water levels in the rivers drop and so do, the amount of supplies boats can bring. The rainy season means supplies are easier to get, but it also brings strong currents and dangerous conditions.

Christian singers raise their voices and arms in song.

Kano Mosque in northern Nigeria

Religion

About half of all Nigerians are Muslim. They pray five times a day and gather in mosques on Friday, the sacred day of prayer. On holy days Muslims do not eat from dawn to dusk.

Forty percent of the country is Christian. Catholic Portuguese traders brought the religion with them in the fifteenth century. The rest of the country still follows traditional African religions. Members of the Aladura Church combine Christianity with some of the old beliefs in many different gods and in the creator Ọlọ́run.

Many Nigerian children study in open-air classrooms.

School & Sports

Schools are free and open to all children ages six to fifteen. Many Nigerian adults cannot read or write, so it is especially important for children to get a good education.

Soccer, which Nigerians call football, is the country's most popular sport. People of all ages play games in fields, on street corners, or in any open space. Nigeria's national soccer team is called the Super Eagles. The country also has a women's team called the Super Falcons.

Soccer is Nigeria's favorite sport.

Traffic jams are common in Lagos!

Transportation

Many Nigerians depend on boats to travel from place to place and to get essential supplies. Others use cars and trucks. Lagos is a bustling city full of millions of people, winding streets, and more than a few traffic jams. Many times, vehicles come to a complete stop, and then crawl along, inch by inch, in what Nigerians call go-slows.

kiss

(kiss)
when one car bumps into another in a traffic jam.

29

A Yoruba shrine in the Sacred Forest

Unusual Places

About 140 miles (225 km) north of Lagos is the city of Oshogbo. Oshogbo is known for its annual Ọshun Festival and the Ọja Ọba Market. But Oshogbo's most famous site is the Sacred Forest. Here visitors can see huge sculptures and shrines dedicated to a number of Yoruba gods.

Cloth peddler selling his wares

Visiting the Country

Kano's Kurmi Market is one of the oldest and largest markets in Africa. It sells everything from baskets and boxes brimming with fresh fruits and vegetables, to pottery, clothing, leather, and metal.

Visitors may enjoy a trip to Yankari National Park, about 550 miles (885 km) from Lagos. The majority of Nigeria's wildlife lives here, including lions, elephants, hippos, and crocodiles. Bumpy truck rides are offered, as are slower, quieter walking tours.

These musicians in Argungu are playing traditional Nigerian drums.

Window to the Past

Music has played an important part in Nigeria's history. Ancient artifacts and bronze plaques show musicians playing traditional drums, horns, bells, and **lutes.**

Music has always been an important part of Nigerian life.

Later, European and American music became influential, as did the fast beat of **calypso.** Jùjú music began in the 1940s, and then in the 1970s, Afro-Beat evolved. Afro-Beat combined African rhythms with American soul music. Many Nigerian songs during this time were about politics and people's rights.

Today, Nigerians listen to a wide variety of music, including traditional jùjú and Afro-Beat, as well as modern-day rap, jazz, and gospel.

Traditional Nigerian
bush hut

X-tra Special Things

The ancient walls of Benin City were covered with elaborate sculptures.

Detail of Benin City wall sculpture

The world's third-largest mangrove forest is in Nigeria. Mangroves are trees that grow in salt water. They have tall roots that grow aboveground. Nigerians use the wood to build houses and the leaves to make roofs.

About seven hundred years ago, a huge, elaborate system of moats and walls was built in and around Benin City. Originally, the walls were almost 60 feet (18 m) tall and spread out over hundreds of square miles! Today, many of the walls have collapsed or have been torn down. Enough remain, however, to give people a real peek into the past.

Muslims at a festival called a durbar

Yearly Festivals

Nigerians celebrate a number of holidays, depending on their religion. Christians celebrate Good Friday, Easter, and Christmas. Muslims gather at least twice a year at festivals called durbars, when people ride and race horses, dance, sing, and wear traditional costumes. Ethnic groups hold traditional festivals to honor their ancestors or to ensure a good harvest.

The Sokoto River is jam-packed during the Argungu Fishing Festival.

During the Argungu Fishing Festival, hundreds of fishers rush into the Sokoto River and try to catch as many fish as they can with nets, dried gourds, or even their hands!

This fisherman has his nets ready!

Farmers move their herds along railroad tracks in modern-day Zaria.

Zaria

Ganuwar Amina

(gAA-nUU-wAr A-mI-nA)
means "Amina's walls."

The city of Zaria is found in the northern part of Nigeria. Much of it is covered in the puffy, soft white blossoms of cotton plants. Zaria is known for growing peanuts, as well as cotton. Once called Zazzau, the city is home to more than 369,000 people and several colleges.

Long ago, Zaria was ruled by a queen named Amina Zazzua (1533-1610). Amina ruled the area until her death at age seventy-seven. She introduced the idea of building walls around military camps for protection. Some of these walls still exist today!

Nigerian and English Words

calypso a type of music with an emphasis on beat and humorous lyrics

composer a person who writes, or composes, music

dictators absolute rulers or tyrants

extinct no longer living

geometrical using simple geometric forms such as circles and squares in design and decoration

lutes stringed instruments with a long neck and a pear-shaped body lengthwise

mosques Muslim houses of worship

plantains fruits that look like bananas but are eaten cooked

savannas areas of grassland with scattered trees

silt fine particles of soil washed by flowing water into a river or lake

terra-cotta a type of dried clay often used to make pottery

Let's Explore More

Bikes for Rent! by Issac Olaleye, Orchard Books, 2001

The Magic Tree: A Folktale from Nigeria by I. Obinkaram Echewa, Morrow Junior Books, 1999

Nigeria (Cultures of the World) by Patricia Levy, Benchmark Books, 2004

Nigeria—The People by Anne Rosenberg and Bobbie Kalman, Crabtree Publishing, 2001

Websites

http://www.cia.gov/cia/publications/factbook/geos/ni.html
This Web site from the *CIA World Factbook* provides you with numbers and important facts about the entire country.

http://www.worldalmanacforkids.com/explore/nations/nigeria.html
This Web site from the *World Almanac for Kids* gives great information on the land, economy, education, and history of Nigeria.

Index

Italic page numbers indicate illustrations.

Meet the Author

TAMRA ORR is a full-time writer and author living in Portland, Oregon. She has written fifty nonfiction books for children and families. Many of them have been about different places all over the planet, including *Slovenia, Turkey,* and *Taiwan* for Scholastic, and *New Jersey, Colorado, Barbados,* and *Windward Islands* for other publishers. In 2004, one of her books won the New York Public Library's Best Nonfiction Book for Teens award. In addition to books, Orr writes articles for magazines and also works for several national standardized testing companies.

Orr graduated from Ball State University in Muncie, Indiana. In the fall of 2001, she and her husband and four children (ages eight to twenty) moved across the country from Indiana to Oregon. Her children teach her something new every single day.